MW01122720

ISBN 0-9726861-1-8

Laserfiche
A Division of Compulink Management Center, Inc.
3545 Long Beach Blvd.
Long Beach, CA 90807
USA

Third edition
Printed in the USA

Contents

Introduction

"We can deliver loans much faster with this new system, and it will greatly reduce the cost to process, close and ship the home loans. These savings can greatly reduce the cost of home ownership."

Steve Harry, Senior Vice President,
Harry Mortgage

The purpose of this guidebook is to provide an understanding of how the right document management solution can make your organization more profitable and efficient, as well as to provide basic guidelines for solution evaluation, selection and regulatory compliance.

From banks to insurance firms, investment firms, CPAs and other public companies, the cost of complying with recordkeeping-related regulations continues to rise. In this increasingly stringent regulatory environment, a document management solution's ability to mitigate expenses while also facilitating compliance with applicable rules has become a crucial consideration.

Beyond compliance, two other important issues to investigate when considering document management solutions are the nature of the software itself and the commitment of the firm you choose to install and support it.

The vendor you choose to facilitate your transition to digital document management will play a major role in the overall success of your investment. The vendor must make the commitment to learn how your organization currently organizes documents, what type of information your firm files and retrieves, as well as the specific rules and regulations to which your firm must adhere.

Paper, Compliance and the Bottom Line

The Growing Paper Problem

"Each day, U.S. workers generate 2.7 billion new sheets of paper."

ATG & Rheinner, Reuters, 1996

We all need it to do our work, but paper accumulates quickly, and no one knows this better than those in the financial services industry. Keeping up with all the paper is more than a full-time job...

Not only the paper you may generate...

- Buy/sell orders
- Applications
- Illustrations and presentations
- Correspondence
- Meeting notes

But the incoming paper from...

- Loan applications
- Appraisals
- Fund/investment statements
- Transaction confirmations
- Correspondence
- Applications
- Quarterly statements
- Commission statements
- Newsletters
- Reference materials
- 401k information
- Tax returns
- Wills and trusts
- Medical records

For example, even a small investment firm with 450 to 500 clients could be looking at a minimum of 75,000 new sheets of paper each year. Multiply that times 100 or 1,000 or many thousands for large firms or banks, and you have a massive repository of paper you cannot destroy. As the amount of paper grows, businesses are paying the price. Paper files are often hard to find, easy to lose and costly to reproduce and distribute. Studies show that professionals often lose up to 500 hours a year looking for documents.

Although the actual percentage of documents printed will decline from 90 percent today to about 40 percent in 2005, Richard Thoman, CEO of XEROX, noted, in absolute numbers, that still represents a fourfold growth in printed page volume, to 4 trillion pages annually.

Business Wire, January 18, 2000

Paper and Profitability

U.S.-based companies spend...$25 to $35 billion processing (filing, storing and retrieving) paper. Management of documents over their life cycle pushes that figure up to $100 billion a year.

IDC, January 1997

Information industry estimates show that a typical worker will take 12 minutes to process a single document. Nine of these 12 minutes are spent searching for, retrieving and refiling the document. Only three minutes are spent using the information.

In 1995, Coopers and Lybrand released a study that showed that the average office:

- Makes 19 copies of each document.
- Spends $250 recreating each lost document.
- Spends $20 on labor for filing each document.
- Loses 1 out of 20 office documents.
- Spends $120 searching for every misfiled document.
- Spends $25,000 to fill a 4-drawer file cabinet and $2,000 annually to maintain it.

The volume of paper documents that corporations must process has increased tenfold in the last five years. Increase in paper volume drives the cost of paper handling higher, which reduces profit margins.

According to a 2000 report from the Seattle-based firm of Moss Adams, the average financial planner's office is consumed by inefficiencies and excessive overhead. Moss Adams notes, "Firms with multiple practitioners spend 42.4% of annual revenues on overhead expenses, leading to a 4% after-tax profit. The most costly operating expenses are other salaries (9.9% of gross profit) and rent (5.2%)."

Take a close look at your organization and consider:

- What are the costs and legal risks of managing regulatory compliance with paper files?
- How much time is lost searching for client files or customer information?
- How many hours are lost due to not having information easily available?
- How much money and time are lost copying, mailing and faxing documents?
- How much is spent on storage space?
- What would happen to your information in the event of a disaster?
- What is the cumulative impact of all these on your profitability and quality of customer service?

Document management gives you the power to recapture lost hours, reduce your overhead expenses and increase profitability, while improving the level of service you provide to your customers. Time saved can be devoted to cultivating new customers and generating additional revenue.

Going Paperless

Document and Records Management Defined

Digital document management systems are software applications that capture paper and electronic documents and provide storage, retrieval, security and archiving for those documents. Records management is a specialized discipline. In particular, it is a set of recognized practices related to the life cycle of records – information that serves as evidence of the business activities of an organization.

Your organization generates large amounts of paper and electronic documents. Traditional methods of storing paper and electronic records require a great deal of effort to manage, distribute and find those documents. As files grow in number, the time and effort required to manage them also increases.

Document management revolutionizes the management of information and provides the ability to rapidly find, retrieve and share all documents in your system. Document management systems for the financial services industry should have eight basic characteristics:

- Capture tools to bring documents into the system
- Methods for archiving and storing documents
- Ability to support compliance requirements
- Indexing systems to organize documents
- Retrieval tools to find documents
- Tools for mining information in paper documents and repurposing existing data
- Access controls to provide documents only to authorized staff
- Disaster recovery tools

Internet usage has grown exponentially due to the vast amounts of information it provides access to. Similarly, document management systems prove to be tremendously valuable because they provide fast access to the information within your important documents.

Document management leverages the value of paper documents. Files are scanned or electronically converted and a high-resolution image is saved on any storage media. Files can still be viewed, printed, shared and stored, but document management adds an enormous advantage by giving documents active content and enabling advanced applications, such as automated workflow routing.

No longer just ink on a page, document text is read by optical character recognition (OCR) technology. Any document management system should allow you to retrieve files by searching for any word or phrase in the text, by folder location or by index card information. The very best systems will allow you to find documents using a combination of all three methods.

A document management system should also provide comprehensive security to protect customer and client information from unauthorized access. When the time comes for system expansion, scalability is essential, as is the ability to integrate seamlessly with existing applications.

Records management systems simplify the life-cycle management of business records. A records management system supports the automatic enforcement of consistent, organization-wide records policies and reduces the cost of regulatory compliance.

Records management software provides:

- Improved efficiency in the storage, retention and disposition of records and record series.

- Detailed reports of which records are eligible for transfer, accession or destruction.

- Audit trails to track all system activity and the entire life cycle of records.

The Department of Defense 5015.2-STD has become the de facto standard for records management software across a wide spectrum of industries. DoD 5015.2 outlines the baseline functionality required for the records management applications used by the U.S. Department of Defense and has been endorsed by the National Archives and Records Administration (NARA). Records management applications that have been certified as DoD 5015.2 compliant provide the peace of mind that comes from objective, third-party evaluation.

The Benefits of Going Paperless

By implementing a truly interactive document management system through a carefully structured implementation plan, your firm should realize these benefits:

Instant retrieval

Digital document management lets you find documents quickly, without leaving your desk. Paper and microfilm are slower because users must go to storage rooms and filing cabinets to search for information manually.

Simultaneously share documents

Document management systems make it easy to share documents electronically with colleagues and clients over a network, on CD or securely through the Web. Sharing paper documents usually entails photocopying, and sharing microfilm documents requires conversion to paper.

Reliable digital archiving

Your files are maintained in a secure, unalterable state that can be backed-up to WORM or CD-ROM storage media.

Reduce storage space needs

By converting paper to digital images, you reduce the need to store paper. You reduce or eliminate not only the filing cabinets in your office, but also boxes of files that may be stored off-site. A single CD-ROM can hold up to 10,000 pages, the equivalent of a 4-drawer filing cabinet.

Reclaim productive time

Instead of searching for information, your time is now better spent meeting the needs of your current customers and acquiring new ones.

Increase profitability

Your firm should be able to minimize overhead costs while maximizing productivity and efficiency.

Eliminate document loss

OCR technology allows you to dramatically reduce document loss and misfiling by reading and indexing each word in every document.

Improve security

With paper files, the only security control you have is to lock the filing cabinet. Document management provides the ability to restrict access to sensitive documents and redact portions of a document that others may not be permitted to see.

Disaster recovery

If paper files burn or are lost in a flood, they are gone forever. With document management you can quickly recover from any disaster, as all of your document images, index cards and vital information can be archived on and restored from CD-ROM or backup tape.

Streamlined Workflow

Solutions with an automated workflow option deliver more efficient and cost-effective document-centered work processes. A workflow solution reduces costly paper handling with intelligent document routing within the document management system. Workflow also improves accountability with automatic notification of action and inaction.

Regulatory Compliance

A solution that is flexible enough to help you maintain compliance in an evolving regulatory environment is key to mitigating the risk of non-compliance. Your solution should also reduce costs associated with paper record-keeping and facilitate producing records on demand to auditing authorities.

How Document Management Works for Financial Services

"Laserfiche provided us with the modern tools that, today, greatly reduce our paper flow and add efficiency to our processing of paper-based information. Also, we are prepared for the state and federal bank regulators to review our document management and records retention policies, and that's an important factor for any new bank."

John Blecher, CFO, York Traditions Bank

Nearly all financial services organizations utilize computers to perform daily operations. By implementing a comprehensive document management system, you eliminate your dependence on paper files in the office and on the road.

You may be able to review policy or account information from software packages you currently utilize, but in many cases you still do not have online access to all the information that is on the paper documents.

Document management captures the complete document with no retyping required and turns all of the words on that piece of paper into an active database of information, providing something better than a paper file.

What can you digitize?

Paper documents can be scanned, while all electronic files can be imported and printed into your document management system, including:

Applications
Buy/Sell Tickets
Charts
Checks
Client Invoices
Commission Statements
Correspondence
Daily Receipts
Financial Statements
401k Information and Files
Graphs
Hand-Written Notes
Illustrations
Loan Documents
Medical Records
Mortgage Documents
Order Confirmations
Photographs
Proposals
Presentations
Purchase Orders
Quarterly Statements
Reports
Tax Returns
Vendor Invoices
Wills and Trusts

Organization and Daily Use

Organize files in the same manner as your current filing system. Maintain separate files for clients, staff, customers, pending applications, reference information, etc.

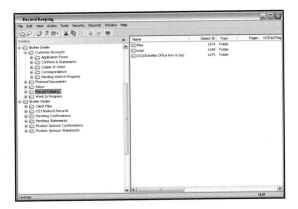

Intuitive Visual Interface

You are able to maintain separate folders and documents according to the preferred procedures to which you are accustomed.

For example, financial planners are able to maintain compliance by preserving separate files for Life Insurance, Qualified and Non-Qualified.

Effective document management solutions allow you to store scanned documents and electronic documents, such as word processing and spreadsheet files, in their native formats, all within the same folder.

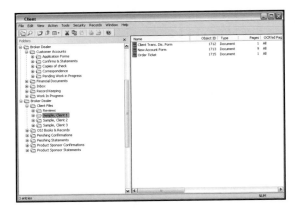

Easy File Viewing

You should be able to easily view your documents with a wide variety of options. Open the document to see a single page clearly and legibly...

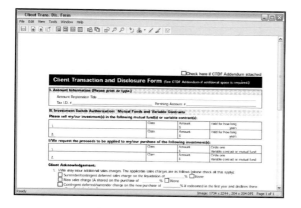

...or open with the thumbnail view to see all the pages in the document.

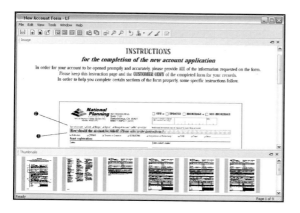

Add to Existing Files

To add pages to an existing document, simply open the folder, click Scan and instruct the software how to place the page – as the first page, the last page or somewhere in the middle.

Quick Shortcuts to Files

Using a document managment system for active files eliminates the clutter on desks and floors and eliminates the need to leave your desk to get information from the file cabinet. You can establish working files for each staff member and then drag the active folder that you are working on into the staff member's folder.

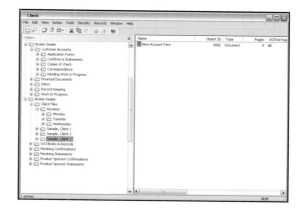

For example, for client reviews, you can easily set up a review folder and drag the client's file there, so that all information is readily available to you and the client.

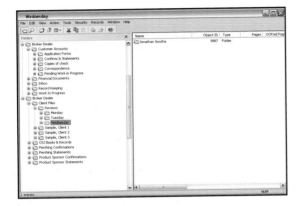

Add Working Comments

Use sticky notes within the document management system for notes regarding what needs to be done on a particular case or for reminders of what information you are looking for.

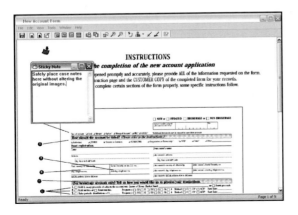

Easy to Move Documents

When papers are misfiled manually, it is often nearly impossible to find them again, especially on short notice.

Within a document management system, you can instantly find any document by searching for words in the document. If a document is misfiled, you can simply drag the document to the proper folder.

Print Directly to Your Files

You can establish files that include proposals, research and illustrations that you created through other software programs.

There is no need to print a paper copy for your files, because you can simply import the reports directly to your document management system and into the appropriate folder.

Custom Stamps

With your entire mission-critical repository of loan documents, mortgage documents and other essential records in your document management system, you can use custom stamps to indicate actions such as Reviewed, Approved, etc.

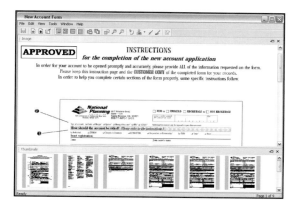

Indexing

Indexing allows you to quickly and effectively cross-reference information, as well as provide other means for narrowing your document searches.

Indexes are custom-designed to meet your specific needs, so you are not restricted by a predefined format. Indexes can store a variety of information including, but not limited to, Creation Date, Client Name, Type of Account, Fund Company or Loan Type, Representative's name, Account numbers, Social Security numbers and Account Status.

A convenient feature of indexes is that you do not have to enter information every time you scan supporting documents into an existing file. The indexes are set at the document level, meaning that, if you are adding new pages to a document, you simply append the original document.

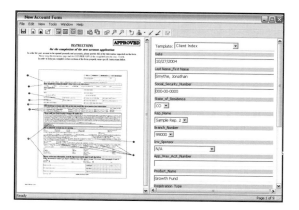

OCR

Optical Character Recognition enables you to find any document based on a single word, phrase or combination of words contained within a document.

OCR reads every word in your documents and indexes them automatically – so when it comes time to retrieve documents, they are found quickly and easily.

Search and Retrieval

Intuitive search capabilities such as full-text indexing, fuzzy logic and index cards allow documents to be retrieved instantly. This eliminates long, time-consuming manual searches for information through a filing cabinet or pile of papers. OCR turns the words on paper documents into active content – a database of invaluable information at your fingertips created without any data entry.

A full-featured document management solution easily traces historical information on any account or customer. You can digitize archival documents, as well as current/active files, eliminating your need to call up records from an off-site storage facility in search of an elusive piece of information.

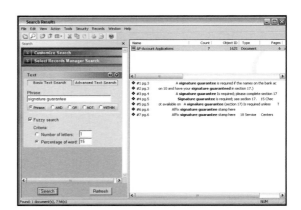

Search results should give you the ability to target the information you need quickly, zeroing in on the exact line of a given document.

Distribution

Once you have stored your documents in a secure digital archive, you can simply e-mail or fax the information directly to your home office, fund company or loan administrator. If you need a hardcopy of the information, you can simply print the files from your document management system.

Document management allows you to share files within your office, simultaneously and without the need to generate photocopies. This enables two or more people to work on the same file from the comfort of their desk at the same time, something that you can't do with paper.

For example, if you are heading out of the office for a client meeting, there is no need to take a hardcopy file with you. You can take all of the information you need, including the entire history of the client, on your notebook computer or a CD-ROM.

Superior document management systems provide a secure Web distribution solution as well. Authorized staff and clients can access critical information from around the office and around the world. You can browse, search, view and print any document with standard Web browsers, just as if you were in your office. Publishing documents to the Web should be a dynamic process that is easily managed without HTML coding.

Security

You can control who has access to your files, what content they view and what functions they perform. You can add annotations, including highlighting, stamps and sticky notes to your documents, or you can redact portions of a document to prevent unauthorized access to confidential information.

Audit trails monitor every action within the system, providing a detailed history of every stored document. You have complete control over your documents, something that is nearly impossible to duplicate with paper files.

To protect you against any possible disaster, complete CD-ROM backups of your entire digital archive, including images, indexes and the databases can be stored off-site, with duplicate copies made available at your local office.

Compliance

Securities & Exchange Commission (SEC)

National Association of Securities Dealers (NASD)

Internal Revenue Service (IRS)

Federal Deposit Insurance Corporation (FDIC)

Health Insurance Portability and Accountability Act (HIPAA)

Sarbanes-Oxley Act (Also known as the Corporate Reform Act)

Gramm-Leach-Bliley (Also known as the Financial Modernization Act)

USA PATRIOT Act

In an increasingly demanding regulatory environment, a document management solution not only improves the bottom line, but also helps limit exposure to civil and criminal liability due to non-compliance.

It is important to realize that technology itself cannot guarantee compliance. The essence of compliance lies in the application of systematic policies and procedures established by your organization to maintain, protect and provide access to business-essential records. To be truly valuable as a compliance tool, technology must be flexible and secure enough to support the complex recordkeeping procedures required in a multi-regulatory environment.

The above list is a sampling of the regulations and entities whose policies impact your document and records management procedures. When evaluating document management systems, keep in mind that the solution's capacity to facilitate compliance is central to its success.

While laws and auditing authorities vary by industry and region, you will find most regulations have many points in common with regard to electronic recordkeeping. Two basic principles underlie many of the regulations. First, you must set the information in time. This means that the date and time that images are digitally created on your system are recorded and cannot be changed. This relates directly to the second issue, which is that the storage media your system uses must be unalterable.

On the following page are basic guidelines that can help your organization eliminate paper files while maintaining regulatory compliance. Of course, your solution provider should work closely with your compliance officers to make sure your solution helps avoid the risks of non-compliance while streamlining auditing, third-party storage and other compliance-related recordkeeping procedures.

Basic Compliance Guidelines

• You must be able to retrieve records on demand.

• Your images and database must be stored on acceptable media.

• You must maintain your records in an unalterable format.

• You must be able to store your documents on unalterable media (i.e., CD-ROM, DVD), or you must deploy audit trail tracking that clearly identifies the original dates that all images were captured into your system.

• For financial planners, a copy of your records must be maintained by a third party, independent from your operation. Copies must be readily available to auditors, when requested.

• A complete and accurate transfer of records can be made.

• Your system must have reasonable controls to ensure integrity, accuracy and reliability.

• Your system has reasonable controls to prevent and detect unauthorized creation of, addition to, alteration of or deletion of records.

• Your system has reasonable controls to prevent and detect records deterioration.

• Your system must have an indexing system that facilitates document retrieval.

• Your system has the ability to print copies of records when required.

• Your system must be able to cross-reference with other recordkeeping systems and software.

• Your system must have documentation on how the software works and how it is set up.

Implementation:
Addressing Your Business Needs

Evaluation Criteria

Ease of Use

Any software system must be easy to use for all users within the organization. This means that those with the least amount of computer experience easily can use the software to complete their daily tasks.

Organization

A document management system should not force you to change the way you work to fit its requirements. Rather, the document management system should be adaptable to your specific needs.

You need a document management system with the flexibility to emulate your current filing system. You need the ability to see your documents in a file folder structure and the ability to move your documents from one folder to another. Many document management systems rely solely on database searches to get you the documents you need and do not provide a visual way to organize documents. This is like throwing your documents in a filing cabinet without file folders and expecting to find the exact information you need by reaching in and choosing files at random.

Additionally, the system must allow you to easily add new documents to an existing file or folder. You do not start a new folder for every new piece of paper that you receive for a client, and you should not have to do so with a document management system.

Bringing in documents

A full-featured document management system will allow you multiple ways to capture your documents. While scanning is key, you should not be forced to print everything before you can store the documents in your system. Your document management system should provide the ability to import faxes and e-mails and support electronic documents in their native formats.

Think of how long it takes to find information regarding a customer. Not just paper documents, but information stored in computers – word-processing files, spreadsheets, presentations and illustrations.

Imagine how efficient it would be to store all information, paper and electronic, in one place while providing enterprise-wide access. Document management systems provide that benefit.

Scanners

The quality of your scanner and the image capturing software it uses will play a major role in your ability to create high-quality images.

Without a quality scanner, your images will not OCR well, making your documents harder to find when you need them most. When looking at scanners, there are several factors that you should take into consideration:

Duplex: If the majority of the documents that you receive are double-sided, a duplex scanner is a necessity. This will reduce the amount of time required to scan documents into your document management system.

DPI: This means dots per inch and relates to the quality of the image stored on your computer. The lower the DPI, the lower the resolution, and the harder it will be to OCR and retrieve documents. To ensure better OCR quality, the minimum scanner setting should be 300 dpi.

ADF: Automatic Document Feeder. Like a copier, the ADF allows you to stack several pieces of paper on the scanner at once, rather than feeding one piece of paper at a time.

Speed: The faster the speed, the higher the price tag. However, you must weigh the speed of the scanner with the volume of documents received on a daily, weekly and monthly basis. While a slower scanner may be a lower initial investment, it could cost you more in personnel time.

Paper Sizes: Make sure that you get a scanner that can handle the majority of paper sizes that your office deals with. Most scanners can handle 8 1/2-inch x 11-inch and 14-inch x 11-inch paper. If you use or store wide ledger sheets (11 inches x 17 inches) or smaller statement or check-size pieces of paper, your scanner must be able to accommodate them.

Search and Retrieval

Your document management system should provide several ways to quickly and easily find documents. A visual search method is extremely important in making sure that all personnel within the office are comfortable with the software and can quickly see the documents that they want.

A full-text search for words or phrases is important to not only find specific documents, but also to cross-reference large amounts of data quickly and efficiently.

Advanced Boolean searches enable you to customize the exact search criteria and give you more flexibility in how you find and cross-reference information quickly.

Index searches allow you to find documents with specific index information, again providing an excellent means of finding a group of documents quickly and efficiently.

And finally, the ability to utilize a combination of various searches is essential in narrowing down the search options and increasing retrieval speed.

Distribution

Whether you need to send a copy of your documents to another office or to a staff member in your building, document distribution should be easy and efficient. If all members of your office are networked, document distribution should be instant and automatic. If you need to send copies of documents across town or across the nation, an e-mail interface, fax interface and Web interface are important features that will save you time and money. Why have a document management system if you need to print a hardcopy just to share the information?

Backup and Archival

The ability to store your documents in their original state is not only a compliance issue, but also a practical necessity, and one of the major benefits of a document management system.

Backups of your document management system should include more than just images. They should also contain all database and index information. Tape backups are effective for backing up large blocks of information from a computer, but publishing your data to a CD-ROM provides greater flexibility and a very effective means of recovering lost data and getting back to business quickly in the event of an emergency.

Compliance rules and regulations from NASD SEC, IRS, FDIC and others dictate that images must be maintained in their original state and must be stored on an unalterable format, such as CD-ROM, DVD, or WORM.

An important issue regarding CD-ROM, DVD and WORM backup is making sure that the information is completely useable once it is stored on the media. Storing encrypted TIFF images and text on a CD-ROM does not provide good usability. The better choice is to publish a CD that includes the associated images, text files, database and most importantly a viewer, thus making the CD-ROM a completely accessible medium.

Security

The ability to control access to sensitive documents should be of primary importance when examining a document management system.

A document management solution should provide the ability to set access-level security based on groups of people as well as specific individuals. It should allow you to control what an individual can do with the documents, (i.e. scan, print, e-mail, view, retrieve, delete, and move).

A secure document management system should enable you to control what information on a document can be viewed by whom, and what information is extremely sensitive. The ability to redact portions of a document ensures optimum security for you and your clients. An audit trail should also be available to track user activity.

Open Architecture

With the multitude of software applications used in the office environment today, you need a document management system that has the ability to easily share information with your other applications. Open architecture is critical to the ability of your document management solution to integrate with other business-essential applications.

On the Road

If your job takes you out of the office, your document management system should be able to go with you. Whether you are traveling locally or around the world, chances are you will need documents with you. A document management system should provide the ability to take files with you electronically.

Implementation Plan

When document management systems fail, it is often because there was not a comprehensive plan in place.

Your implementation plan should examine your specific needs and equipment requirements, installation, training, back-file and active file conversion, document conversion if converting from one system to another, and database maintenance. It should outline how the system should be utilized to best serve your organization.

Milestones and target dates should be established and most importantly, a backup plan should be created to account for any problems that could arise.

Support

Whomever you purchase your document management system from should understand your business and your goals. The vendor should become an active partner in your solution and your success.

The firm you choose should not only understand document management, but should also understand the intricacies of your industry and your operation. It should make the commitment to learn your specific needs and how you utilize your files on a daily, weekly and long-term basis. This is one of the major keys to your success.

Look for a firm that provides complete solutions. Talk with the firm's clients and find out if the firm is truly responsive to customers' needs. Does the firm provide real solutions or merely stock answers that don't really resolve problems? Will the firm be there when you need it?

Software Updates

With constantly evolving computer hardware and software technology, you want to make sure that you purchase software from a firm that offers regularly scheduled software updates and enhancements.

Investigate whether software updates are offered under a maintenance and support agreement or if you have to purchase them separately. Find out how often software updates are released, and how they will be installed on your system. If the vendor makes a major release, it is important to find out if you will get the new release under your agreement, or if you will have to repurchase the software.

Software updates, enhancements and bug fixes help ensure that you will receive the best possible performance and quality from your document management investment.

Implementation Guidelines

Careful planning is one of the most important elements of a successful implementation. Planning needs to begin before the first dollar is spent on the project. Projects have a much better chance of success if someone has documented, in detail, the project scope, system requirements, schedule, business case and technical environment before you begin. As obvious as it may sound, these first steps are frequently not accomplished until the project has already started.

The vendor you choose as your document management consultant should assist you in the creation of a document management implementation plan. If you try to do this in-house, without the assistance or experience of trained professionals, you may miss important elements that would greatly affect the success and cost of your document management system implementation.

When it comes time to put your document management system to work for you, a pilot project is one way to begin. Have your staff review the progress and make sure that the conversion from paper to paperless is working for you. If changes need to be made, it is much better for your operation and your staff when they are made upfront.

The following implementation guidelines will help you get started:

Clearly Identify Your Goals and Objectives

- What do you expect a document management system to do for you?
- What problems do you need to solve?
- How do you plan on using the system?
- Do you need the document management system to interface with current business-critical applications?

Needs Analysis

- How many people will need access to the files?
- How many people will be scanning in paper?
- Do you currently have a network in place?
- Do you require new computers?
- Do you require computer upgrades?
- How many scanners will be required?
- What capabilities will you need?
- Where does the majority of your paper originate?
- What is the weekly amount of new paper coming into your office?
- Do you need audit trails or CD publishing?
- What are the retention schedules for the documents you store?
- Determine the size requirements for your system by counting the number of filing cabinets and storage boxes you have now, as well as the number of new pieces of paper that come into your office on a daily, weekly and annual basis.

Document Distribution

- Do you need to fax or e-mail documents?
- Do you have offices in various locations that require copies of your records?
- Do you need to take your documents out of the office?

File Structure and Indexes

- How do you look up information?
- What type of information will be stored in the system?
- What type of cross-referenced information do you need?
- How many different indexes do you need?

Daily Procedures

- Who will perform the scanning operations?
- What types of information are to be scanned?
- What are the workflow procedures?
- What should be done with the paper after it is scanned?

How should you proceed with your new document management system from day one?

Conversion from microfiche or other management systems

- Who will do the conversion?
- How long will it take?
- How much will it cost?

Back-File Conversion

- 100% or partial?
- Determine what archived records need to be converted.
- How many archived records do you need to convert?
- Who will perform the conversion?
- How long do you need to retain these records?
- Does your office ever refer to these records? How often?
- How long will it take to complete the process?

Day-Forward

- Only scan records from this day forward?
- What if you need old documents in storage?
- What types of information should be scanned?
- Who will perform the scanning?

On-Demand Day-Forward

- Back files are scanned only when required.
- The amount of back files decrease over time.

Real-World Success Stories

Financial Planner Boosts Productivity, Facilitates Compliance

BINGHAM AND HENSLEY, a certified financial planning organization in Kingsport, Tennessee, had serious problems with its existing document management system and wanted a solution.

"We are in our files on a daily basis, and there was no way to easily see the individual files for any given client and no way to easily maintain the separate file folder structure of Life Insurance, Non-Qualified and Qualified folders as dictated by our compliance regulations," said Jeff Bingham. "We were and are solely dedicated to going paperless, but our system at the time was not living up to expectations and not giving us the solution that we needed."

After an extensive search of the various document management systems on the market, they became quick fans of Laserfiche the minute they saw how its visual file folder structure could emulate their existing filing system. Not only could Laserfiche be utilized to store their archival records, but, by scanning new pages into an existing client file folder, Bingham and Hensley could maintain active client files within Laserfiche. The use of the Laserfiche sticky note pad enabled them to make comments on documents or files within Laserfiche, just as they would store handwritten notes in a paper-bound client file.

In addition to storing paper documents in Laserfiche, Bingham and Hensley stores illustration and proposal client records directly in Laserfiche. Now when they want to recall a specific proposal that was created in any of their financial planning software toolkits, they can quickly access the records and database from one manageable location — the Laserfiche client file.

Bingham and Hensley's short-term goals were to eliminate their seven filing cabinets and scores of storage boxes. The long-term projection is to be able to provide more efficient service to their clients, spend less time finding files and information and to be fully compliant with all federal and corporate regulations.

"John Caso and Alternative Data Imaging have taken the time to learn our filing system, what our specific needs are, and assist us in developing an implementation plan that will enable us to realize our goals," said Jeff Bingham. "Without a doubt that is probably one of the biggest keys to a successful document imaging system."

CPA Firm Streamlines Accounts Payable and Receivable Operations

Kennedy and Coe, the 56th largest CPA firm in the nation, is using Laserfiche to help its headquarters organize and archive Accounts Payable, Accounts Receivable, and General Ledger information.

Kennedy and Coe, headquartered in Salina, Kansas, has 23 offices scattered throughout Kansas, Colorado, Nebraska and Oklahoma. Any invoice coming into those offices must be paid through the Accounts Payable office located at headquarters.

The Accounts Payable office handles more than 100 invoices a week. In the past, once the invoice was received and paid, it was kept on file for a year, then sent downstairs for storage. If a question came up about an invoice, someone would have the arduous task of searching for it.

"An invoice from several years back could take days to find in the basement," Greg Davis, Associate and IT Director of Kennedy and Coe, said. If a satellite office had a question about an invoice, it would have to be found, copied and mailed or faxed to them, taking up valuable time and company resources.

"With Laserfiche I can look up the invoice myself in a matter of seconds," Davis said. Employees at Kennedy and Coe can utilize Laserfiche's advanced folder structure to pull up information, or its search capabilities to pull up a document based on a template or keyword search. "Once our Accounts Payable person receives and pays an invoice, she scans it into Laserfiche and shreds it. If anyone needs the information, they can look it up in Laserfiche. The satellite offices can now call and get the invoice emailed immediately without having to wait," Davis said.

Laserfiche was installed as a pilot program — part of the company's overall decision to go paperless. "One of our offices is nearly paperless already," Davis said. "We felt Laserfiche would fit our needs in taking the company records paperless."

Implementation began with the administration department. Davis said the firm plans to move it into every department and eventually grant select staff in the home office and satellite offices access to company records. The next step is to make employee data paperless. Laserfiche's comprehensive security allows access only to those with rights granted by the administrator to view specific folders, documents and even information on a specific document.

The company uses a Citrix server for the satellite offices to access programs and data at the main office. Remote office staff are able to utilize Laserfiche as easily as those in the home office do.

Bank Delivers Superior Customer Service and Maintains Compliance

York Traditions Bank is living up to its promise to deliver a technology-driven operation along with customer-first values. With the help of Laserfiche, the brand-new bank is well on its way to every clerk's dream: a paperless office.

With 101 years of collective experience, the bank's senior leadership knew which technologies kept their promises and which ones went unused. The new bank needed to cast an eye toward the future without compromising its ability to meet stringent SEC and FDIC regulations. The Laserfiche database holds millions of scanned documents, while built-in security features provide management and customers with peace of mind.

The bank also needed a solution provider to implement Laserfiche and integrate its many benefits with a reliable management system. They didn't have to go beyond the local yellow pages to find one. A local authorized Laserfiche reseller dispatched a team of engineers to design an integrated program that combined easy-to-use Laserfiche technology with industry-standard bank management software.

"Laserfiche provided us with the modern tools that, today, greatly reduce our paperflow and add efficiency to our processing of paper-based information," said John Blecher, the bank's chief financial officer. "Also, we are prepared for the state and federal bank regulators to review our document management and records retention policies, and that's an important factor for any new bank."

York Traditions Bank scans and electronically archives a majority of its paper documents. Clerks can use full-text retrieval to find documents within seconds, while built-in security features protect customers' private financial information.

Insurance Firm Cuts Labor Costs, Improves Information Access

Thousands of paper policy documents instantly found their way to underwriters' computer screens as Bloss & Dillard, Inc. aggressively implemented a paperless system.

The Huntington, West-Virginia-based managing general agent (MGA) represents more than 1,500 independent agents throughout four states. Bloss & Dillard handles a wide range of risks, from simple property to highly sophisticated excess and umbrella coverage. IT manager Tate Tooley wanted a way to make 350,000 documents easily accessible.

As each of the 7,000 policies entered the Laserfiche system, Laserfiche Quick Fields™ technology automatically sent the digital documents to the appropriate underwriters. Within hours, the same policies that once required a deep dig through a file cabinet now were a mouse click or two away.

After batch-processing the old documents, Tooley set up Quick Fields to automatically route new policies, e-mail and faxes in the same manner. A paperless mail system soon replaced the mail cart.

"Many of our clients had switched to digital documents and the paperless office in recent years, so we were a little out of date with our paper filing system," Tooley said. "The key was to mold this new system to our current workflow pattern, with minimum lag time during the integration process."

Quick Fields also reduced labor costs that would have been associated with such an ambitious project. Without Quick Fields, staff would have had to manually find each folder after scanning it into Laserfiche. Quick Fields saved 20 minutes per policy, which factored out to approximately $23,000 worth of saved labor costs.

Helping a Mortgage Banker Swim Upstream

OKLAHOMA CITY – Steve Harry, senior vice-president of Harry Mortgage, knew he had to rethink the way he managed everyone's information in such a paper-intensive business. Filing cabinets storing hundreds of documents on each application filled the second floor of the company's two-story headquarters in Oklahoma City. "One floor for our papers, one for our people," Harry joked.

To improve records accessibility, the company reengineered its records system to create a paperless office with Laserfiche. Instead of storing paper records in manila folders, personnel scan them into a computer system with a hard drive capable of storing 1.8 million files in the space now occupied by a single cabinet. With Laserfiche, each file can be called up for study on any one of 50 workstations with a few keystrokes.

The speed of the Laserfiche system is a big advantage for moneylenders: the faster the delivery, the less danger there is that interest rates will change while the documents are in transit.

"We can deliver loans much faster with this new system, and it will greatly reduce the cost to process, close and ship the home loans. These savings can reduce the cost of home ownership," Harry said.

Frequently Asked Questions

General

Q. What is a document?

A. A document consists of information stored on anywhere from one to several thousand pages. It can include images and/or text, plus annotations, and one template (index card).

Q. Can I edit or alter images?

A. A document management system should not allow the original image to be altered or edited. Annotations should be overlays that do not alter the original document. It is important to protect the original image in order to maintain both the legal status of the document and the integrity of the system.

Q. Do document management systems support audit trails?

A. Yes. A document management system's audit trail should record username, date, time, document name and action for every instance in which a user accesses a database or document. Various levels of audit trail logging detail and activity tracking should be available. The system should include a viewer to sort and filter these logs. Audit trails are especially important for regulatory compliance.

Q. What is the standard format used to store images?

A. Black and white images are most commonly stored as standard TIFF files using CCITT Group IV (two-dimensional) compression. Grayscale and color images are frequently stored as TIFF files with JPEG compression.

Q. What is the standard format used to store text?

A. ASCII, which stands for the American Standard Code for Information Interchange, has been the standard, non-proprietary text format since 1963.

Q. How much disk space does a document management system typically require?

A. A single page typically occupies around 50KB of disk space, if the image is stored in TIFF Group IV. Each gigabyte (GB) of storage space, which amounts to only a few dollars, holds approximately 20,000 pages. With the significant drop in prices for hard drives and optical media, it costs much less to store documents in a document management system than on paper.

Q. What if my database is too big to fit in one data volume?

A. A document management system should allow data and images to be stored across multiple volumes, with each volume residing in a different directory or on a different drive, disk array, CD or MO disk.

Capture

Q. What are the most common hardware and software scanner interfaces?

A. Many scanners attach to an Adaptec SCSI card or to a Kofax Image processing board. Most scanners use either TWAIN or ISIS scanner drivers to communicate with the computer.

Q. How can I scan forms?

A. Forms processing components often use multiple OCR engines and elaborate data validation routines to extract hand-written or poor-quality print from forms that go into a database. Because many forms that are scanned were never designed for imaging or OCR, it is essential to have good quality assurance mechanisms in place when scanning forms to correct errors that might occur.

Q. Can I capture information from multi-function peripherals (MFPs)?

A. A full-featured document management system allows you to capture documents from different network locations, including MFPs, or devices that perform any combination of scanning, printing, faxing or copying.

Q. How can I scan large format documents?

A. Several manufacturers make scanners specifically designed for large format documents up to E-size (34 inches x 44 inches) and A-0 size (33 inches x 46.8 iches). If you do not have one of these, the document can be reduced in size using a photocopier and then scanned with a normal scanner, or sent to a service bureau that has large format scanners.

Q. What image resolution should I use?

A. Most imaging systems can support documents scanned at various resolutions, from 50 dpi to 600 dpi (or more) depending on your scanner. Depending on the purpose and the contents of the page, most documents are scanned in black and white at 300 dpi.

Q. What about color files or photographs?

A. Imaging systems should support black and white, grayscale and color images. Color files can be scanned with a color scanner or imported into a document management system. There are a wide range of color scanners on the market. Many document management scanners support color and grayscale.

Q. How can I scan double-sided documents?

A. An imaging system should provide two different ways to do this. It should support duplex scanners, which simultaneously scan both sides of a page, and simplex scanners, which require the user to scan all the front sides, place the documents in upside down and then scan all the back sides, before the system collates the pages into the correct order.

Q. Can I scan landscape and portrait pages together?

A. An imaging system should allow you to change the orientation of pages during or after scanning. A well-designed system will also include an option to automatically check and correct the orientation of pages.

Q. How are skewed images handled?

A. Skewed (crooked or tilted) images can adversely affect the accuracy of the OCR process, so an imaging system should include software that recognizes skewed images and compensates for them. This is particularly important when scanning press cuttings on a flat bed scanner or when scanning documents through a worn-out or poorly designed automatic document feeder (ADF).

Q. How can I scan checks?

A. Several manufacturers make scanners specifically designed for checks, which read the magnetically encoded MICR (Magnetic Ink Character Recognition) numbers at the bottom of the check. If you do not have one of these scanners, most checks can be scanned with regular document imaging scanners and OCR-processed as usual, though the MICR numbers will not be read. To integrate MICR information into the document management database, the document management system must support check scanning hardware.

Q. What file formats can a versatile system import?

A. A versatile system should be able to import the files you encounter in your office. This includes word processing files, spreadsheets and presentations as well as common image formats such as TIFF Group IV, TIFF Group III, TIFF Raw, TIFF LZW, PCX, BMP, CALS, JPEG, GIF, PICT, PNG and EPS Preview images. A document management system providing long-term archival of documents should allow the images of each page to be stored in a non-proprietary format. For example, electronic document pages would be printed to the document management system, black and white graphical files would be converted to TIFF Group IV format and color/grayscale images would be converted to TIFF or JPEG.

Indexing

Q. How do I index scanned documents?

A. There are three primary ways to index documents: folder structure, index or template fields, and full-text indexing. Folder structure essentially functions as a visual indexing method that allows users to browse for documents by categories. Index or template fields categorize documents according to keywords, which can be either manually entered or automatically assigned by the document management program. Full-text indexing is the automated process of entering every word in a document into the index.

Q. What is OCR?

A. OCR stands for Optical Character Recognition and refers to the way a computer converts words from an unsearchable scanned image to searchable text. OCR is usually necessary in order to use full-text indexing and searches, so it should be included in an imaging and document management system. OCR engines can generally only recognize typed or laser-printed text, not handwriting.

Q. What is the difference between OCR and indexing?

A. OCR is the process of converting scanned images to text files. Full-text indexing is the process of adding each word from a text file to an index that specifies the location of every word on every document. Well-designed document management software can make this a fast and easy procedure, providing rapid access to any word in any document.

Q: What is the difference between index field searches and full-text searches?

A: Index field or template searches enable you to retrieve preestablished categories of documents, whereas full-text searches turn up every occurrence of designated words in the database. When the database contains a large number of documents, the difference between sorting documents by topic and listing every occurrence of a word in the database – including passing references – is significant in terms of the time required to analyze the search results and locate the desired document(s).

Q. How accurate is OCR?

A. Accuracy on a freshly laser-printed page is typically better than 99.6%. Accuracy on faxed, dirty or degraded documents will be lower, so it is essential that an imaging system have image clean-up technology to improve OCR accuracy.

Q. Do I have to go through text to correct OCR mistakes manually?

A. Well-designed systems allow users to correct OCR errors from within the system. However, when hundreds or thousands of pages are scanned every day, it is usually not practical to clean up the text. Because the OCR process does not have perfect accuracy, it is important that the document management system support fuzzy logic searches. Fuzzy logic searches allow for misspelling and will find words even if the OCR engine makes occasional mistakes.

Q. How fast is the OCR process?

A. The performance of the OCR and indexing processes is entirely dependent on factors such as the speed and configuration of the host system as well as the contents of the image.

Q. What is ICR (Intelligent Character Recognition)?

A. ICR is pattern-based character recognition and is also known as Hand-Print Recognition. Handwritten text is more difficult for computers to recognize and results in higher error rates than printed text. ICR engines usually do best at recognizing constrained printing, which means block printed letters with one letter in each box. Accurate recognition of unconstrained handwriting, especially cursive handwriting, typically requires that the ICR engine be trained to recognize each user's style of writing.

Q. What is OMR (Optical Mark Recognition)?

A. OMR, also called Mark-Sense Recognition, is the recognition of marks commonly used on forms, such as check marks, circled choices and filled-in bubbles. OMR can be an important part of a document management system for organizations that process many standard forms. Exam forms and customer survey cards are perhaps the best-known examples of OMR.

Q. Can OCR-processed text be exported and reused in a word processor?

A. Yes, you can usually cut and paste text between the document management system and another Windows application, or you can export complete text files (all text pages in a document) to a directory and open it with your preferred word processing program.

Viewing/Printing/Exporting

Q. Can I open and display more than one document at a time?

A. Some document management systems will allow you to display multiple documents, with the number of documents that you can have open simultaneously limited only by the amount of memory available.

Q. How can I resequence pages of a document before printing or exporting?

A. If pages are out of order and need to be resequenced, a well-designed document management system will allow you to drag thumbnail views of pages to the required position. In the same way, individual pages can be selected and deleted, subject to appropriate security access control and privileges.

Q. What is the advantage of a large monitor?

A. For people who use an imaging system frequently, screen size can be a critical factor. If users are to flip between pages with the ease of real paper, they must be able to view the whole page at once in a way that allows the text to be readable. If $8^1/_2$-inch x 11-inch pages are the dominant paper size, then a 21-inch monitor capable of displaying 1600 x 1200 is optimal. Using a 15-inch VGA monitor will require scrolling and panning if the image is viewed at normal size.

Q. What other display considerations are important?

A. Screen resolution and the refresh rate of the monitor are also important. Generally, the larger a monitor is and the higher resolution it has, the harder it is to get the high refresh rate that is required for sustained viewing without screen flicker. The optimum threshold for minimum flicker is generally considered to be a horizontal refresh rate of 72 MHZ on a 21-inch monitor. The maximum refresh rate is a function of the monitor and the graphics controller.

Q. Will I need a specialized printer for images or OCR-processed text?

A. Generally no. Most imaging systems support a wide variety of Windows-compatible printers, but an optimal configuration includes a laser printer with at least 4 MB of RAM. If you are using a networked system and printing high volumes of pages to a network printer, you might consider installing a separate laser printer either locally or on its own network segment to minimize network traffic.

Q. In which formats can I export documents?

A. It depends on the document management system. Common graphical formats include TIFF Group III, TIFF Group IV, TIFF Raw, BMP, PCX, PNG and JPEG.

Q. What happens when a user without redaction viewing rights prints a document that has been redacted?

A. A document management system should protect the integrity of the document by printing with the redactions intact.

Records Management

Q. Are all documents records?

A. No. Records management is a specialized discipline that deals with information serving as evidence of an organization's business activities. In particular, it is a set of recognized practices related to the life cycle of that information. Often, records refer to documents, but they can include other forms of information, such as photographs, blueprints or even books.

Q. What does records management software do?

A. Records management software supports the application of systematic controls to the creation, maintenance and destruction of an organization's records.

Q: Does DoD 5015.2 certification guarantee compliance with other regulations like HIPAA?

A. No. It is important to distinguish between regulatory compliance and the DoD 5015.2 standard. The DoD standard represents baseline functionality for records management applications (RMAs) used within the Department of Defense. It serves as the de facto standard for records management applications across government and industry. However, it is a records management standard and not a broad regulatory compliance standard. DoD-5015.2 certification facilitates compliance by supporting the application of systematic records policies; it cannot however er guarantee compliance. Compliance is a process dependent on the application of records policies.

Q: How do records management applications help enforce proper polcies?

A: Records management applications can support the application of consistent policies and procedures through a series of mechanisms, including: mandatory metadata acquisition and automated extraction of e-mail metadata; support for time, event and time-event dispositions; automated notification for review of vital records; freezing of records; and comprehensive audit trail reporting.

COLD (Computer Output to Laser Disc)

Q. What is the difference between COLD and imaging?

A. COLD is specifically for archiving, indexing, searching and printing reports from high-volume text files generated by mainframes, mini-computers and other computer applications. COLD stores large report files and extracted index fields on hard disk, optical cartridge or CD-ROM instead of printing all the information out on paper or storing it to microfilm.

Q. How many index fields can the COLD server extract from each report?

A. The number of index fields is usually unlimited. However, the more fields extracted from each report, the more slowly the extraction process will run and the larger the index files will be.

Conclusion

With the greater availability and acceptance of document imaging technology, along with the rapidly declining cost of computer systems, hard drives and accessories, the productivity and efficiency gains and profitability enhancements make a document management solution a prudent investment.

In this environment, a document management solution is a business-essential aspect of day-to-day operations. It is a solution that cuts costs, reclaims storage space for revenue-generating activities, allows staff to redirect labor to more productive tasks and simplifies compliance with ever-changing regulations.

A document management system should be flexible enough to adapt to your operation and address the needs of multiple departments. A scalable, open architecture system allows you to start small and expand your solution as your needs change.

Document management solutions can work effectively in a single, one-person office, all the way up to a company with a staff of thousands. The key is getting the system that's right for your organization.

Please call (800) 985-8533 or (562) 988-1688 x 125 to find out what document imaging can do for your organization, or visit **www.laserfiche.com/fs** for more information.

Glossary of Terms

Access Rights

A security mechanism that lets the system administrator determine which objects (folders, documents, etc.) users can open. It should be possible to set access rights should for groups and individuals.

ADF

Automatic Document Feeder. This is the means by which a scanner feeds the paper document.

Annotations

The changes or additions made to a document using sticky notes, a highlighter or other electronic tools. Document images or text can be highlighted in different colors, redacted (blacked-out or whited-out) or stamped (e.g., FAXED or CONFIDENTIAL), or have electronic sticky notes attached. Annotations should be overlaid and not alter the original document.

ASCII

American Standard Code for Information Interchange. Used to define computer text that was built on a set of 255 alphanumeric and control characters. ASCII has been a standard, non-proprietary text format since 1963.

ASP (Active Server Pages)

A technology that simplifies customization and integration of Web applications. ASPs reside on a Web server and contain a mixture of HTML code and server-side scripts. An example of ASP usage includes having a server accept a request from a client, perform a query on a database and then return the results of the query in HTML format for viewing by a Web browser.

Audit Trail

An electronic means of tracking all access to a system, document or record, including the modification, deletion and addition of documents and records.

Bar Code

A small pattern of lines read by a laser or an optical scanner, which correspond to a record in a database. An add-on component to document management software, bar-code recognition is designed to increase the speed with which documents can be stored or archived.

Batch Processing

The name of the technique used to input a large amount of information in a single step, as opposed to individual processes.

Bitmap/Bitmapped

See Raster/Rasterized.

BMP

The abbreviation for a native file format of Windows for storing images called bitmaps.

Boolean Logic

The use of the terms AND, OR and NOT in conducting searches. Used to widen or narrow the scope of a search.

Briefcase

A method to simplify the transport of a group of documents from one computer to another.

Burn (CDs or DVDs)

To record or write data on a CD or DVD.

Caching (of Images)

The temporary storage of image files on a hard disk for later migration to permanent storage, like an optical or CD jukebox.

CD or DVD Publishing

An alternative to photocopying large volumes of paper documents. This method involves coupling image and text documents with viewer software on CDs or DVDs. It is essential that search software be included on the CDs or DVDs to provide immediate retrieval abilities.

CD-R

Short for CD-Recordable. A CD that can be written (or burned) only once. It can be copied as a means to distribute a large amount of data. CD-Rs can be read on any CD-ROM drive whether on a standalone computer or network system. This makes interchange between systems easier.

CD-ROM

Compact Disc-Read Only Memory. Written on a large scale and not on a standard computer CD burner (CD writer). An optical disc storage medium popular for storing computer files as well as digitally recorded music.

Client-Server Architecture vs. File-Sharing

Two common application software architectures found on computer networks. With file-sharing applications, all searches occur on the workstation, while the document database resides on the server. With client-server architecture, CPU-intensive processes (such as searching and indexing) are completed on the server, while image viewing occurs on the client. File-sharing applications are easier to develop, but they tend to generate tremendous network data traffic in document management applications. They also expose the database to corruption through workstation interruptions. Client-server applications are more difficult to develop, but dramatically reduce network data traffic and insulate the database from workstation interruptions. See also n-Tier Architecture.

COLD

Computer Output to Laser Disc. A process that outputs electronic records and printed reports to laser disc instead of a printer. Can be used to replace COM (Computer Output to Microfilm) or printed reports such as green-bar.

COM

Computer Output to Microfilm. A process that outputs electronic records and computer generated reports to microfilm.

Compression Ratio

The ratio of the file sizes of a compressed file to an uncompressed file. With a 20-to-1 compression ratio, an uncompressed file of 1 MB is compressed to 50 KB.

Deshading

Removing shaded areas to render images more easily recognizable by OCR.

Deskewing

The process of straightening skewed (off-center) images. Documents can become skewed when they are scanned or faxed. Deskewing is one of the image enhancements that can improve OCR accuracy.

Despeckling

Removing isolated speckles from an image file. Speckles can develop when a document is scanned or faxed.

Disposition

Actions taken regarding records after they are no longer required to conduct current business. Possible actions include transfer, archiving and destruction.

Dithering

The process of converting grays to different densities of black dots, usually for the purposes of printing or storing color or grayscale images as black and white images.

Document Management

Software used to store, manage, retrieve and distribute digital and electronic documents, as well as scanned paper documents.

DoD 5015.2-STD

The Department of Defense (DoD) 5015.2 standard. Represents the standard for evaluating electronic records management applications (RMAs) used within the DoD. The standard has been endorsed by the National Archives and Records Administration (NARA).

Duplex Scanners vs. Double-Sided Scanning

Duplex scanners automatically scan both sides of a double-sided page, producing two images at once. Double-sided scanning uses a single-sided scanner to scan both pages, scanning one collated stack of paper, then flipping it over and scanning the other side.

DVD

Digital Video Disc or Digital Versatile Disc. A disc similar to a CD, on which data can be written and read. DVDs are faster, hold more information and support more data formats than CDs.

Feature Rights

A security mechanism that allows system administrators to determine the actions that users can perform on the objects to which they have access.

Flatbed Scanner

A flat-surface scanner that allows users to capture pages of bound books and other non-standard-format documents.

Folder Browser

A system of on-screen folders (usually represented as hierarchical, or stacked) used to organize documents. For example, the Windows Explorer program in Microsoft Windows is a type of folder browser that displays the directories on your disk.

Forms Processing

A specialized document management application designed for handling preprinted forms. Forms processing systems often use multiple OCR engines and elaborate data validation routines to extract hand-written or poor quality print from forms to go into a database. With this type of application, it is essential to have good quality assurance mechanisms in place, since many of the forms that are commonly scanned were never designed for imaging or OCR.

Full-Text Indexing and Search

Enables the retrieval of documents by either word or phrase content. Every word in the document is indexed into a master word list with pointers to the documents and pages where each occurrence of the word appears.

Fuzzy Logic

A full-text search procedure that looks for exact matches as well as similarities to the search criteria, in order to compensate for spelling or OCR errors.

GIF

Graphics Interchange Format. CompuServe® 's native file format for storing images.

Gigabyte (GB)

2^{30} (approximately one billion) bytes, or 1024 megabytes. In terms of image-storage capacity, one gigabyte equals approximately 17,000 $8^{1}/_{2}$-inch x 12-inch pages scanned at 300 dpi, stored as TIFF Group IV images.

Grayscale

An option to display a black-and-white image file in an enhanced mode, making it easier to view. A grayscale display uses gray shading to fill in gaps or jumps (known as aliasing) that occur when displaying an image file on a computer screen.

ICR

Intelligent Character Recognition. A software process that recognizes handwritten and printed text as alphanumeric characters.

Image Enabling

Allows for fast, straightforward manipulation of an imaging application through third-party software. For example, image enabling allows for launching the imaging client interface, displaying search results in the client and bringing up the scan dialogue box, all from within a third-party application.

Image Processing Card (IPC)

A board mounted in the computer, scanner or printer that facilitates the acquisition and display of images. The primary function of most IPCs is the rapid compression and decompression of image files.

Index Fields

Database fields used to categorize and organize documents. Often user-defined, these fields can be used for searches.

Internet Publishing

Specialized document management software that allows large volumes of paper documents to be published on the Internet or intranet. These files can be made available to other departments, offsite colleagues or the public for searching, viewing and printing.

ISIS and TWAIN Scanner Drivers

Specialized applications used for communication between scanners and computers.

ISO 9660 CD Format

The International Standards Organization format for creating CD-ROMs that can be read worldwide.

JPEG

Joint Photographic Experts Group (JPEG or JPG). An image-compression format used for storing color photographs and images.

Key Field

Database fields used for document searches and retrieval. Synonymous with index field.

MFP

Multifunction Printer or Multifunctional Peripheral. A device that performs any combination of scanning, printing, faxing, or copying.

Multipage TIFF

See TIFF.

Near-Line

Documents stored on optical discs or compact discs that are housed in the jukebox or CD changer and can be retrieved without human intervention.

n-Tier Architecture

When applied to the physical or logical architecture of computing, refers to a method of distributed computing in which the processing of a specific application occurs over n number of machines across a network. Typical tiers include a data tier, business logic tier and a presentation tier, wherein a given machine will perform the individualized tasks of a tier. Scalability is among the advantages of n-tier architecture.

OCR

Optical Character Recognition (OCR). A software process that recognizes printed text as alphanumeric characters. OCR enables full-text searches of documents and records.

Off-Line

Archival documents stored on optical discs or compact discs that are not connected or installed in the computer, but instead require human intervention to be accessed.

On-Line

Documents stored on the hard drive or magnetic disk of a computer that are available immediately.

Open Architecture

Applied to hardware or software whose design allows for a system to be easily integrated with third-party devices and applications.

Optical Discs

Computer media similar to a compact disc that cannot be rewritten. An optical drive uses a laser to read the stored data.

Pixel

Picture Element. A single dot in an image. It can be black and white, grayscale or color.

Portable Volumes

A feature that facilitates the transfer of large volumes of documents without the need to copy multiple files. Portable volumes enable individual CDs to be easily regrouped, detached and reattached to different databases for a broader information exchange.

Raster/Rasterized (Raster or Bitmap Drawing)

A method of representing an image with a grid (or map) of dots or pixels. Typical raster file formats are GIF, JPEG, TIFF, PCX, BMP, etc.

Record

Information, regardless of medium, that constitutes evidence of an organization's business transactions.

Record Series

A record series is a group of records subject to the same set of life-cycle instructions.

Redaction

A type of document annotation that provides additional security by concealing from view specific portions of sensitive documents, such as particular words or phrases. Like all annotations in a document imaging system, redactions should be image overlays that protect information but do not alter original document images.

Region (of an image)

An area of an image file that is selected for specialized processing. Also called a zone.

Retention Period

The length of time that a record must be kept before it can be destroyed. Records not authorized for destruction are designated for permanent retention.

Scale-to-Gray

See Grayscale.

Scalability

The capacity of a system to scale up, or expand, in terms of document capacity or number of users without requiring major reconfiguration or re-entry of data. For a document management system to be scalable, it must be easy to configure multiple servers or add storage.

Scanner

An input device commonly used to convert paper documents into computer images. Scanner devices are also available to scan microfilm and microfiche.

Security Markings or Tags

Within records management applications, a security-based metadata field intended to define and restrict access, as well as facilitate classification and retrieval.

SCSI Scanner Interface

The device used to connect a scanner with a computer.

Single-Page TIFF

See TIFF.

SQL

Structured Query Language. The popular standard for running database searches (queries) and reports.

Templates, Document

Sets of index fields for documents.

Thumbnails

Small versions of an image used for quick overviews that give a general idea of what an image looks like.

TIFF

Tagged Image File Format. A non-proprietary raster image format, in wide use since 1981, which allows for several different types of compression. TIFFs may be either single or multi-page files. A single-page TIFF is a single image of one page of a document. A multi-page TIFF is a large, single file consisting of multiple document pages. Document management systems that store documents as single-page TIFFs offer significant benefits in network performance over multipage TIFF systems.

TIFF Group III (compression)

A one-dimensional compression format for storing black and white images that is utilized by most fax machines.

TIFF Group IV (compression)

A two-dimensional compression format for storing black-and-white images. Typically compresses at a 20-to-1 ratio for standard business documents.

Versioning

In document or records management applications, the ability to track new versions of documents after changes have been made.

Workflow, Ad Hoc

A simple manual process by which documents can be moved around a multi-user document management system on an as-needed basis.

Workflow, Rules-Based

A programmed series of automated steps that routes documents to various users on a multi-user document management system.

WORM Disks

Write-Once-Read-Many Disks. A popular archival storage medium during the 1980s. Acknowledged as the first optical discs, they are primarily used to store archives of data that cannot be altered. WORM disks are created by standalone PCs and cannot be used on the network, unlike CD-Rs. In some industries, such as financial services, the definition of WORM has broadened to include other media, such as CD-ROMs and DVDs, which provide accessible but unalterable document storage.

Zone OCR

An add-on feature of document management software that populates document templates by reading certain regions or zones of a document and then placing information into a document index field.

Acknowledgments

Information in this booklet has been gathered from various sources, including but not limited to:

ARMA newsletters

AIIM newsletters

Studies published by Coopers & Lybrand

Business Wire

Imaging Magazine

Gartner Group Research Publications

ATG & Rheinner, Reuters

2000 FPA Financial Performance and Compensation Survey of Financial Planning Practitioners by Moss Adams

John Caso of Alternative Data Imaging, Johnson City, Tennessee

Jim Starcev, Etelligent Consulting

Document Imaging for the New Millennium, a Laserfiche publication

Compliance, Technology & the Paperless Office, a Laserfiche presentation

About Laserfiche

Since 1987, Laserfiche has created simple and elegant document management solutions that help organizations run smarter. Laserfiche solutions manage mission-critical information and records in over 21,000 local, state and federal agencies; educational institutions; healthcare organizations; financial services firms; and other public- and private-sector organizations around the world.

The Laserfiche development team is a skilled and experienced group of professionals who are well rounded in both the theoretical and practical aspects of programming and document management. Laserfiche strives to bring a far-reaching business perspective to each new project, helping solve customer problems through:

- Objectivity
- Experience
- Understanding the various business processes at work in different industries and organizations

Laserfiche combines knowledge of real-world working systems with technological expertise in order to create solutions that lead to better working environments.

Laserfiche welcomes the opportunity to answer further questions about document management and to arrange Web or on-site demonstrations of Laserfiche document management solutions.

For more information, contact:
info@laserfiche.com

Laserfiche
3545 Long Beach Blvd.
Long Beach, CA 90807
United States

Phone: 562-988-1688
Toll-free: 800-985-8533 (within the U.S.)
Fax: 562-988-1886
www.laserfiche.com